Shaken, 93 Martini Cocktail Recipes

Gourmet Goodness Kuro

Copyright © 2023 Gourmet Goodness Kuro
All rights reserved.
:

Contents

INTRODUCTION 7
1. Classic Martini 9
2. Dirty Martini 9
3. Gibson Martini 10
4. Vesper Martini 10
5. Espresso Martini 11
6. French Martini 12
7. Chocolate Martini 13
8. Lemon Drop Martini 13
9. Apple Martini 14
10. Peppermint Martini 15
11. Vanilla Martini 15
12. Cosmopolitan Martini 16
13. Mango Martini 17
14. Pineapple Martini 17
15. Watermelon Martini 18
16. Blueberry Martini 19
17. Grapefruit Martini 19
18. Raspberry Martini 20
19. Blackberry Martini 21
20. Spiced Pear Martini 22
21. Cucumber Martini 22
22. Ginger Martini 23
23. Lavender Martini 24
24. Hibiscus Martini 24
25. Elderflower Martini 25
26. Rose Martini 26
27. Cardamom Martini 26

28. Peach Martini 27
29. Apricot Martini 28
30. Strawberry Martini 28
31. Orange Martini 29
32. Tangerine Martini 30
33. Fig Martini 30
34. Honey Martini 31
35. Pomegranate Martini 32
36. Plum Martini 33
37. Rhubarb Martini 33
38. Melon Martini 34
39. Kiwi Martini 35
40. Lychee Martini 35
41. Coconut Martini 36
42. Hazelnut Martini 37
43. Almond Martini 38
44. Pistachio Martini 39
45. Walnut Martini 39
46. Maple Martini 40
47. Bacon Martini 41
48. Mediterranean Martini 42
49. Mexican Martini 42
50. Italian Martini 43
51. German Martini 44
52. Dutch Martini 44
53. Japanese Martini 45
54. Chinese Martini 46
55. Indian Martini 47
56. Thai Martini 47

57. Brazilian Martini 48
58. Russian Martini 49
59. Irish Martini 49
60. Scottish Martini 50
61. Caribbean Martini 51
62. African Martini 51
63. American Martini 52
64. Asian Martini 53
65. Oceanic Martini 54
66. Vegetarian Martini 54
67. Vegan Martini 55
68. Gluten-free Martini 56
69. Low-carb Martini 57
70. Keto Martini 57
71. Paleo Martini 58
72. Dairy-free Martini 59
73. Nut-free Martini 59
74. Soy-free Martini 60
75. Egg-free Martini 61
76. Grain-free Martini 61
77. Sugar-free Martini 62
78. Non-alcoholic Martini 62
79. Mocktail Martini 63
80. Herbal Martini 64
81. Floral Martini 65
82. Fruity Martini 65
83. Nutty Martini 66
84. Sweet Martini 67
85. Sour Martini 67

86. Salty Martini 68

87. Spicy Martini 69

88. Bitter Martini 69

89. Umami Martini 70

90. Dry Martini 71

91. Extra Dry Martini 71

92. Very Dry Martini 72

93. Bone Dry Martini 73

CONCLUSION..74

INTRODUCTION

Shaken, not Stirred: 93 Martini Cocktail Recipes is a cocktail cookbook that celebrates the timeless allure of the martini. With its sophistication, glamour, and versatility, the martini has been the drink of choice for many discerning drinkers for over a century. From James Bond's iconic "shaken, not stirred" catchphrase to its association with Hollywood's golden age, the martini has captured the imagination of cocktail lovers everywhere.

But what exactly is a martini? Traditionally, a martini is made with gin and vermouth, stirred with ice, and strained into a chilled glass. However, the world of martinis has expanded far beyond this classic recipe, with countless variations that use different spirits, mixers, garnishes, and techniques. In this book, you'll find a wide range of martini recipes that cater to all tastes and preferences, from the classic to the contemporary, the sweet to the sour, and the fruity to the spicy.

With 93 recipes in total, Shaken, not Stirred offers something for everyone. Each recipe is accompanied by a full-page photograph that showcases the beauty and elegance of the cocktail, as well as detailed instructions that guide you through the process of mixing, shaking, straining, and garnishing. In addition, the book features tips and tricks on how to make the perfect martini, whether you prefer it shaken or stirred, gin or vodka, dry or wet.

One of the unique features of Shaken, not Stirred is its focus on seasonal ingredients. The book is organized by season, with martini recipes that highlight the flavors and colors of each time of year. From the bright and refreshing Citrus Burst Martini in the summer to the cozy and comforting Holiday Spice Martini in the winter, these seasonal cocktails are perfect for entertaining guests, celebrating special occasions, or simply indulging in a delicious drink at home.

The book also includes chapters on martinis for different occasions, such as brunch, afternoon tea, and dessert. There are also non-alcoholic options for those who prefer a mocktail, as well as tips on how to pair your martini with food. Whether you're a seasoned martini drinker or a novice looking to explore the world of cocktails, Shaken, not Stirred has something to offer.

As the author of this book, I am passionate about creating cocktails that are not only delicious but also beautiful and elegant. My love for martinis began when I was a young bartender, and I found myself drawn to the art of mixology. Over the years, I've experimented with various recipes, techniques, and ingredients, and have discovered that the key to a perfect martini lies in the balance of flavors and textures.

Through this book, I hope to share my passion for martinis with you and inspire you to become a master mixologist in your own right. With its gorgeous photographs, detailed instructions, and wide range of recipes, Shaken, not Stirred is the perfect guide to the world of martinis. So pick up a copy, grab a shaker, and let's get mixing!

1. Classic Martini

Classic Martini: A timeless classic, the Classic Martini is a cosmopolitan libation that is sure to tantalize your taste buds.
Serving: 1
Preparation Time: 5 minutes
Ready Time: 5 minutes

Ingredients:
- 2 oz. London dry gin
- 1/2 oz. dry vermouth
- Dash of orange bitters

Instructions:
1. Fill a shaker with ice.
2. Add the gin, vermouth, and orange bitters to the shaker.
3. Shake the mixture vigorously for 30 seconds.
4. Strain the mixture into a Martini glass, and garnish with an orange peel.

Nutrition Information (per serving):
Calories: 181; Total Fat: 0g; Cholesterol: 0mg; Sodium: 1mg; Total Carbohydrates: 1g; Protein: 0g

2. Dirty Martini

Dirty Martini Cocktail
Serving: 1
Preparation Time: 5 minutes
Ready Time: 5 minutes

Ingredients:
2 ounces Gin (or vodka)
1/2 ounce Dry Vermouth
2 to 3 Olive Brine – the liquid from a jar of olives
1 to 2 Olives

Instructions:
1. In a shaker full of ice, pour in the gin or vodka, vermouth and olive brine.
2. Shake or stir until the outside of the shaker feels cold.
3. Strain the drink into a chilled martini glass.
4. Skewer the olives with a cocktail pick and place in the glass.

Nutrition Information (per serving):
Calories: 170, Total Fat: 0 g, Saturated Fat: 0 g, Cholesterol: 0 mg, Sodium: 332 mg, Carbohydrates: 2 g, Protein: 0 g

3. Gibson Martini

Gibson Martini: This classic twist on the standard Martini makes for an extremely sophisticated and effortless-tasting cocktail.
Serving: 1
Preparation Time: 5 minutes
Ready Time: 5 minutes

Ingredients:
- 3 parts gin
- 3 drops dry vermouth
- 1 slice of pickled onion

Instructions:
1. Place the gin, vermouth, and pickled onion into a shaker filled with ice.
2. Shake vigorously for a few moments to combine the Ingredients.
3. Strain the mixture into a chilled Martini glass.
4. Garnish with a pickled onion.

Nutrition Information:
Calories: 140, Total Fat: 0g, Saturated Fat: 0g, Cholesterol: 0mg, Sodium: 2mg, Carbs: 1g, Protein: 0g

4. Vesper Martini

Vesper Martini: A classic martini made with gin, vodka and Lillet blanc.
Serving: 1
Preparation Time: 5 minutes
Ready time: 5 minutes

Ingredients:
-2 oz gin
-1 oz vodka
-1/2 oz Lillet blanc

Instructions:
1. Add gin, vodka, and Lillet blanc to a cocktail shaker with some ice.
2. Shake until very cold.
3. Strain into a chilled martini glass.
4. Garnish with a lemon twist.

Nutrition Information:
Calories: 132 kcal, Carbohydrates: 0.6g, Protein: 0.1g, Fat: 0g, Saturated Fat: 0g, Sodium: 1.62mg, Potassium: 2mg, Sugar: 0.6g, Vitamin C: 0.1mg, Calcium: 5.2mg, Iron: 0.1mg.

5. Espresso Martini

Espresso Martini is a delightful drink for coffee lovers everywhere. It combines an espresso shot with vodka to create a delicious, energizing cocktail. This version also adds a touch of sugar for a sweet finish.
Serving Size:
Makes 1 cocktail
Preparation Time:
5 minutes
Ready time:
5 minutes

Ingredients:
- 1 oz vodka
- 1 oz espresso
- 1/2 oz sugar syrup
- 2 - 3 coffee beans

Instructions:
1. Fill a shaker with ice and add the vodka, espresso and sugar syrup.
2. Shake until the outside of the shaker is cold.
3. Strain the mixture into a martini glass.
4. Place the coffee beans in the glass and serve.

Nutrition Information (per serving):
Calories: 145, Fat: 0 g, Sodium: 0 mg, Carbohydrates: 9 g, Protein: 0 g

6. French Martini

French Martini
Serving: 1
Preparation Time: 5 minutes
Ready Time: 5 minutes

Ingredients:
- 2 ounces vodka
- 1 ounce pineapple juice
- 1/2 ounce Chambord, or raspberry liqueur
- 1/2 ounce freshly squeezed lime juice
- 1 pineapple slice for garnish

Instructions:
Fill a cocktail shaker with ice cubes. Pour in the vodka, pineapple juice, raspberry liqueur, and lime juice. Shake the Ingredients for about 30 seconds, until the mixture is chilled and the ice cubes have slightly melted.
Fill a martini glass with ice and pour the mix over the ice. Garnish with a pineapple slice and serve.

Nutrition Information:
Calories: 183, Fat: 0g, Sodium: 2mg, Carbohydrates: 11g, Sugar: 7g, Protein: 0g

7. Chocolate Martini

Chocolate Martini is an exquisite, chocolaty version of the beloved classic cocktail. Its smooth and creamy taste makes it a perfect dessert treat for any gathering or special occasion.
Serving: 1
Preparation Time: 5 minutes
Ready In: 5 minutes

Ingredients:
- 1 oz. chocolate liqueur
- 1 oz. vodka
- ½ oz. half and half
- 1 tsp. white sugar
- 1 cherry, for garnish

Instructions:
1. Add the liqueur, vodka, half and half, and sugar to a shaker with ice.
2. Shake the Ingredients together.
3. Pour the mixture through a strainer into a martini glass.
4. Garnish with a cherry or chocolate shavings.

Nutrition Information:
Calories: 180, Fat: 2g, Cholesterol: 5mg, Sodium: 8mg, Carbohydrates: 12g, Protein: 1g.

8. Lemon Drop Martini

Lemon Drop Martini
Serving: 1
Preparation Time: 5 mins
Ready Time: 5 mins

Ingredients:
- 2 oz vodka
- 1 oz limoncello
- Ice cubes
- Fresh lemon wedge

- Simple syrup or sugar

Instructions:
1. Place ice cubes in a shaker.
2. Pour vodka and limoncello in the shaker.
3. Squeeze the lemon wedge and add the juice to the shaker.
4. Add simple syrup or sugar to the shaker and shake everything together.
5. Strain mixture into a martini glass.
6. Garnish with a lemon wedge.

Nutrition Information: (per serving)
Calories: 126 kcal, Carbs: 7.5 g, Protein: 0 g, Fat: 0 g

9. Apple Martini

Apple Martini
  Serving: 1
  Preparation Time: 5 minutes
  Ready Time: 5 minutes

Ingredients:
- 2 ounces vodka
- 1 ounce apple schnapps
- 1/2 ounce freshly squeezed lime juice

Instructions:
1. In a shaker glass filled with ice, add all Ingredients.
2. Shake vigorously for around 10 seconds.
3. Strain the mixture into a martini glass.
4. Garnish the martini with lime or apple slices.

Nutrition Information:
Calories: 173, Total Fats: 0g, Sodium: 0mg, Potassium: 0mg, Total Carbohydrates: 0g, Sugars: 0g, Protein: 0g

10. Peppermint Martini

Peppermint Martini is a light, creamy, and sweet cocktail for special occasions. With a hint of peppermint, this festive martini is a popular choice for meals and special events.
Serving: Makes 1 serving.
Preparation Time: 5 minutes.
Ready Time: 5 minutes.

Ingredients:
- 2 oz vodka
- 2 oz white creme de cacao
- 1/2 cup crushed peppermint candy
- 2 scoops of peppermint ice cream

Instructions:
1. In a shaker filled with ice, combine vodka and white creme de cacao.
2. Stir Ingredients together and strain into martini glass.
3. On a plate, spread crushed peppermint candy and roll the edge of the rim of the glass in the candy.
4. Place two scoops of peppermint ice cream in the center.
5. Enjoy!

Nutrition Information: (for 1 serving, recipe is for 1 serving)
Calories: 567 kcal, Carbohydrates: 61 g, Protein: 2 g, Fat: 16 g, Sodium: 17 mg, Sugar: 42 g.

11. Vanilla Martini

This classic Vanilla Martini is perfect for sipping while unwinding with friends and family. Smooth, creamy and perfectly sweet, this delicious drink is sure to be enjoyed by anyone who loves martinis.
Serving: 1
Preparation Time: 5 minutes
Ready Time: 5 minutes

Ingredients:
- 1 oz vodka

- 0.5 oz. vanilla syrup
- 0.5 oz. cream

Instructions:
1. Fill a shaker with ice.
2. Add vodka, vanilla syrup and cream to the shaker.
3. Shake well.
4. Strain into a chilled martini glass.

Nutrition Information:
Calories: 217 kcal, Carbohydrates: 9.6 g, Protein: 1.1 g, Fat: 1.1 g, Saturated Fat: 0.6 g, Sodium: 4.4 mg, Potassium: 15.7 mg, Fiber: 0.1 g, Sugar: 9.3 g, Vitamin A: 34.6 IU, Vitamin C: 0.1 mg, Calcium: 5.2 mg, Iron: 0.4 mg

12. Cosmopolitan Martini

Cosmopolitan Martini: A classic martini twist on a fruity and flavorful favorite. Serves 1. Preparation time 5 minutes. Ready in 5 minutes.

Ingredients:
- 2 ounces of vodka
- 1/2 ounce of triple sec
- 1/2 ounce of cranberry juice
- 1/4 ounce of fresh lime juice

Instructions:
1. Fill a shaker with ice.
2. Add the vodka, triple sec, cranberry juice, and lime juice to the shaker.
3. Shake the mixture vigorously and strain into a martini glass.
4. Garnish with a lime wedge and enjoy!

Nutrition Information (per serving):
- Calories: 145
- Fat: 0g
- Sodium: 0mg
- Carbohydrates: 4g
- Protein: 0g

13. Mango Martini

This sweet and tart cocktail is the perfect summertime drink, combining mango puree with vodka, orange liqueur and lime juice!
Serving: 1
Prep Time: 5 minutes
Ready Time: 5 minutes

Ingredients:
- 2 ounces vodka
- 1½ ounces orange liqueur
- 1 ounce mango puree
- 1 ounce lime juice

Instructions:
1. Add vodka, orange liqueur, mango puree and lime juice to a martini shaker with ice.
2. Shake vigorously for 30 seconds, or until the outside of the shaker is very cold.
3. Strain the mixture into a martini glass.
4. Garnish with a lime wheel and serve.

Nutrition Information (per serving):
Calories: 187, Total Fat: 0 g, Cholesterol: 0 mg, Sodium: 1 mg, Carbohydrates: 8 g, Dietary Fiber: 0.5 g, Sugars: 5 g, Protein: 0 g

14. Pineapple Martini

Pineapple Martini
Serving: 1
Preparation Time: 5 minutes
Ready Time: 5 minutes

Ingredients:
- 2 ounces vodka
- 1/2 ounce coconut-flavored liqueur

- 2 ounces pineapple juice
- Lime for garnish

Instructions:
1. Fill a shaker with ice.
2. Add the vodka, liqueur, pineapple juice, and lime.
3. Shake vigorously for 15 seconds.
4. Strain the mixture into a martini glass.
5. Garnish with a lime wedge.

Nutrition Information:
Calories: 190, Carbohydrates: 13 g, Protein: 1 g, Fat: 0 g, Sodium: 0 mg, Sugar: 10 g.

15. Watermelon Martini

Enjoy a sweet and refreshing twist to your classic Martini with this Watermelon Martini recipe!
Serving: Makes 2 drinks
Preparation Time: 5 minutes
Ready Time: 5 minutes

Ingredients:
- 3 ounces vodka
- 2 ounces triple sec
- 1/2 cup simple syrup
- 1/2 cup watermelon juice
- Watermelon slice, for garnish

Instructions:
1. In a shaker, combine the vodka, triple sec, simple syrup, and watermelon juice.
2. Shake until combined.
3. Strain the mixture into two glasses.
4. Garnish with a slice of watermelon.

Nutrition Information:

Calories: 180 kcal, Carbohydrates: 15 g, Protein: 0 g, Fat: 0 g, Saturated Fat: 0 g, Sodium: 0 mg, Potassium: 24 mg, Fiber: 0 g, Sugar: 13 g, Vitamin A: 0 IU, Vitamin C: 2 mg, Calcium: 4 mg, Iron: 0 mg

16. Blueberry Martini

Blueberry Martini is a classic cocktail, bursting with bright and juicy blueberry flavor.
Serving: 1
Preparation Time: 5 minutes
Ready Time: 5 minutes

Ingredients:
- 2 ounces vodka
- Juice of half a lime
- 3 ounces cranberry juice
- 5-6 fresh blueberries
- 1 teaspoon of simple syrup

Instructions:
1. Combine the vodka, lime juice, cranberry juice, and simple syrup in a cocktail shaker with ice. Shake until well combined and chilled.
2. Fill a martini glass with ice and strain contents of the shaker into the glass.
3. Place blueberries in the glass and garnish the glass with a lime wedge.

Nutrition Information: Not available.

17. Grapefruit Martini

Grapefruit Martini
Serving: 1
Preparation Time: 10 minutes
Ready Time: 10 minutes

Ingredients:
-3 ounces vodka

- 2 ounces grapefruit juice
- 1 ounce triple sec
- Plenty of ice

Instructions:
1. Fill a martini shaker with plenty of ice.
2. Pour in the vodka, grapefruit juice and triple sec.
3. Shake vigorously until all ingredients are mixed together and the shaker is frosted.
4. Strain into a chilled martini glass.
5. Garnish with a fresh slice of grapefruit.

Nutrition Information:
Calories: 258 kcal
Fat: 0.0 g
Carbohydrates: 11.4 g
Protein: 0.0 g

18. Raspberry Martini

This Raspberry Martini is an acidic, sweet, and perfectly balanced blend of vodka, triple sec, and raspberries. It's the perfect cocktail to enjoy at a party or special occasion.
Serving: 1
Preparation Time: 5 minutes
Ready Time: 5 minutes

Ingredients:
- 1.5 ounces vodka
- 1 ounce triple sec
- 1 ounce raspberry syrup
- 1.5 ounces of fresh lemon juice
- 3 or 4 raspberries

Instructions:
1. In a shaker filled with ice, combine the vodka, triple sec, raspberry syrup, and lemon juice.
2. Shake the Ingredients together for 30-45 seconds.

3. Place one or two fresh raspberries into a martini glass.
4. Strain the mixture from the shaker into the martini glass.
5. Garnish with additional raspberries, if desired.

Nutrition Information: This raspberry martini makes one serving with 153 calories, 0g of fat, 0mg of cholesterol, 3g of carbohydrates, and 0g of protein.

19. Blackberry Martini

Blackberry Martini
Serving: 1
Preparation Time: 5 minutes
Ready Time: 5 minutes

Ingredients:
- 2 fluid ounces vodka
- 1 fluid ounce elderflower liqueur
- 1/4 cup blackberries
- Splash of club soda
- Crushed ice
- Garnish of mint leaves

Instructions:
1. In a cocktail shaker, combine the vodka, elderflower liqueur, and blackberries.
2. Add a handful of crushed ice.
3. Shake for at least 30 seconds.
4. Strain into a martini glass.
5. Add a splash of club soda.
6. Garnish with mint leaves.

Nutrition Information:
Calories: 241; Total Fat: 0.3g, Sodium: 12.0mg, Total Carbohydrate: 12.6g, Sugars: 6.2g, Protein: 0.3g.

20. Spiced Pear Martini

This smooth and robust Spiced Pear Martini is fruity and full of flavor! Serve it as an aperitif or as a fun cocktail at your next party.
Serving: 1
Preparation Time: 5 minutes
Ready Time: 5 minutes

Ingredients:
- 2 ounces vodka
- 1 ounce spiced pear liqueur
- 1/2 ounce fresh lime juice
- Apple and pear slices for garnish

Instructions:
1. Fill a shaker with ice.
2. Pour in the vodka, spiced pear liqueur, and fresh lime juice.
3. Shake vigorously until chilled.
4. Strain the mixed cocktail into a chilled martini glass.
5. Garnish with the fruit slices and enjoy!

Nutrition Information (Per Serving):
Calories: 186 kcal, Carbohydrates: 3 g, Protein: 0.2 g, Sodium: 1 mg, Sugar: 1 g

21. Cucumber Martini

Cucumber Martini is a refreshing and cool martini that is perfect for any summer evening or special occasion. It combines vodka and gin to give it a smooth kick, and the cucumber slices give it a unique and light flavor.
Serving: 1
Preparation Time: 5 minutes
Ready Time: 5 minutes

Ingredients:
- 2 ounces vodka
- 1 ounce gin
- 1 lime wedge

- 3 slices of cucumber
- 1 tablespoon simple syrup
- 2 tablespoons of club soda

Instructions:
1. Fill a shaker with ice.
2. Add the vodka, gin, lime, cucumber slices, and simple syrup.
3. Shake up the Ingredients and strain them into a martini glass.
4. Add the club soda.
5. Garnish with a lime wedge and cucumber slices.

Nutrition Information: Per serving - 250 calories, 0g fat, 35g carbohydrates, 0g protein

22. Ginger Martini

Ginger Martini is a great-tasting twist on the classic martini, home use the cooling refreshing flavors of ginger and citrus to beat the heat.
Serving: 1
Preparation Time: 5 minutes
Ready Time: 5 minutes

Ingredients:
- 1 part Gin
- 1 part Vodka
- 1 part Ginger Syrup
- 1 part Fresh Lemon Juice
- Ginger for Garnish

Instructions:
1. Fill a shaker with ice then add gin, vodka, ginger syrup, and lemon juice.
2. Shake for several seconds, then strain into a martini glass.
3. Garnish with a piece of fresh ginger.

Nutrition Information:
Calories: 128
Fat: 0g

Saturated Fat: 0g
Carbohydrates: 4g
Protein: 0g
Sodium: 0mg
Cholesterol: 0mg

23. Lavender Martini

Lavender Martini
Serving: 1
Preparation Time: 5 minutes
Ready Time: 5 minutes

Ingredients:
- 2 ounces of vodka
- 1 ounce of elderflower liqueur
- 1/2 ounce of simple syrup
- 5-6 lavender sprigs
- 3 drops of lavender essential oil
- Edible lavender petals
- Crushed ice

Instructions:
1. Muddle the lavender sprigs and simple syrup in a shaker cup.
2. Add vodka, elderflower liqueur and essential oil into the cup and shake well.
3. Add crushed ice into a martini glass.
4. Double strain the mixture from the shaker cup into the martini glass.
5. Garnish the martini with edible lavender petals.

24. Hibiscus Martini

Hibiscus Martini is a simple and elegant twist on the classic martini. Delightfully refreshing in flavor, this flavorful martini is sure to make a statement at any gathering.
Serving: 1 martini

Preparation Time: 5 minutes
Ready Time: 5 minutes

Ingredients:
- 2 ounces vodka
- 1 ounce hibiscus syrup
- 2 ounces cranberry juice
- 2 dashes Angostura Bitters

Instructions:
1. In a shaker, combine vodka, hibiscus syrup, cranberry juice, and bitters.
2. Shake until combined and the outside of the shaker is cold.
3. Strain over a martini glass.
4. Garnish with a fresh hibiscus flower, if desired.

Nutrition Information (per serving): Calories: 196, Total Fat: 0 g, Sodium: 2 mg, Carbohydrates: 12 g, Sugars: 11 g, Protein: 0 g.

25. Elderflower Martini

This Elderflower Martini is a tangy and sweet delight, perfect for a warm summer day or as an easy cocktail to impress guests. Featuring elderflower liqueur, lime juice, and a few hardy dashes of dry vermouth, the drink itself is delightfully balanced.
Serving: 2
Preparation Time: 5 minutes
Ready Time: 5 minutes

Ingredients:
- 2 parts elderflower liqueur
- 2 parts lime juice
- 1 dash dry vermouth

Instructions:
1. In a martini shaker filled with ice, add elderflower liqueur, lime juice, and dry vermouth.
2. Shake well.

3. Strain into two martini glasses.
4. Garnish with a slice of lime.

Nutrition Information: Not available.

26. Rose Martini

Rose Martini:
Serving: 1
Preparation time: 5 minutes
Ready time: 5 minutes

Ingredients:
- 2 ounces Rose Vodka
- 1 ounce Elderflower Liqueur
- 1 ounce Grenadine
- 1 teaspoon dry Vermouth
- 2 ounces Sparkling Brut rose Champagne

Instructions:
1. Fill an ice-filled shaker with vodka, elderflower liqueur, grenadine, dry vermouth, and sparkling champagne.
2. Shake vigorously for about 30 seconds, or until the shaker is frosted.
3. Strain into a chilled Martini glass.

Nutrition Information:
Calories: 174, Total Fat 0g, Saturated Fat 0g, Cholesterol 0mg, Sodium 1mg, Carbohydrates 11g, Protein 0g.

27. Cardamom Martini

Enjoy the sweet, floral flavor of Cardamom Martini. This delicious cocktail requires only five simple Ingredients, and can be enjoyed any time of year.
Serving: Serves 1
Preparation Time: 5 minutes
Ready Time: 5 minutes

Ingredients:
- 2 ounces vodka
- 1 teaspoon cardamom simple syrup
- ½ ounce fresh lemon juice
- 1 teaspoon elderflower liqueur
- 1 lemon wheel, for garnish

Instructions:
1. In a shaker filled with ice, combine the vodka, cardamom simple syrup, lemon juice, and elderflower liqueur.
2. Shake vigorously for 30 seconds.
3. Strain into a chilled martini glass.
4. Garnish with a lemon wheel.

Nutrition Information:
Calories: 170, Total fat: 0 g, Sodium: 2 mg, Total Carbohydrate: 4 g, Protein: 0 g

28. Peach Martini

Peach Martini
Serving: 1
Preparation Time: 5 minutes
Ready Time: 5 minutes

Ingredients:
- 2 ounces peach vodka
- 1 ounce peach schnapps liqueur
- 2 ounces orange juice
- 1 ounce fresh lime juice

Instructions:
1. Combine the peach vodka, peach schnapps, orange juice, and lime juice together in a shaker filled with ice.
2. Shake vigorously and strain into a chilled martini glass.

Nutrition Information:

Calories: 202, Fat: 0g, Sodium: 0mg, Sugar: 8g, Carbohydrates: 13g, Protein: 0g

29. Apricot Martini

This tangy-sweet Apricot Martini has a delightful flavor combination of apricot, pineapple, and orange juices, and makes an easy-to-make mixed drink for any social gathering.
Serving: Makes 1 drink
Preparation Time: 5 minutes
Ready Time: 5 minutes

Ingredients:
- 1 to 2 ounces vodka
- 1 ounce apricot nectar
- 2 ounces pineapple juice
- Dash of fresh orange juice
- 2 ounces orange liqueur
- A fresh orange slice

Instructions:
1. Fill a cocktail shaker halfway with ice cubes.
2. Pour in the vodka, apricot nectar, pineapple juice, fresh orange juice and orange liqueur.
3. Shake the Ingredients for 15-20 seconds, or until chilled.
4. Strain the cocktail into a chilled martini glass.
5. Add a fresh orange slice for an attractive garnish.

Nutrition Information: Per serving: 250 calories; 0g fat; 15g carbohydrates; 0g protein.

30. Strawberry Martini

Indulge in this delicious, sweet treat with the Strawberry Martini! This beautiful pink cocktail is made with delicious para-infused vodka and sweet strawberry puree.
Serving: 1

Preparation Time: 5 minutes
Ready Time: 5 minutes

Ingredients:
- 2 ounces raspberry-infused vodka
- 4 ounces sweet strawberry puree
- 1 teaspoon lime juice
- 2 tsp simple syrup
- Lime wedge for garnish

Instructions:
1. In a shaker, add and mix the raspberry-infused vodka, strawberry puree, lime juice and simple syrup.
2. Shake the cocktail well.
3. Pour the drink in a chilled martini glass.
4. Garnish with a lime wedge.

Nutrition Information: Not available.

31. Orange Martini

Celebrate in style with zesty Orange Martini! This delicious beverage is made with orange liqueur, cranberry juice and vodka and is sure to be a hit at your next gathering.
Serving: Makes 1 serving
Preparation time: 5 minutes
Ready time: 5 minutes

Ingredients:
- 2 ounces orange liqueur
- 2 ounces cranberry juice
- 2 ounces vodka

Instructions:
1. In a martini shaker, combine the orange liqueur, cranberry juice and vodka.
2. Fill a shaker with ice and shake the Ingredients together vigorously for 30 seconds or until the outside of the shaker is cold.

3. Strain the drink into a chilled martini glass.
4. Garnish with an orange wedge and enjoy!

Nutrition Information: 155 Calories, 12g Carbs, 0g Fat, 0g Protein

32. Tangerine Martini

Zesty and refreshing, this Tangerine Martini is the perfect pick-me-up after a long day. Easy to make and full of flavor, you'll love sipping on this delicious drink.
Serving: 1
Preparation Time: 5 minutes
Ready Time: 5 minutes

Ingredients:
- 2 parts tangerine vodka
- 1 part triple sec
- 2 parts orange juice
- 1 tablespoon fresh lime juice
- Orange wedge for garnish

Instructions:
1. In a shaker, add tangerine vodka, triple sec, orange juice, and lime juice.
2. Fill the shaker with ice and shake vigorously for about 10 seconds.
3. Strain the mixture into a martini glass.
4. Garnish with an orange wedge.

Nutrition Information:
Calories: 187, Protein: 0.3g, Fat: 0g, Carbs: 16.3g, Sugar: 9.7g

33. Fig Martini

Try this delicious and refreshing Fig Martini that combines vodka, fresh fig puree, Monin Pear Syrup, and fresh lemon juice for a tart, fruity flavor.
Serving: Makes 1 drink

Preparation time: 5 minutes
Ready time: 5 minutes

Ingredients:
- 2oz vodka
- 1oz fresh fig puree
- 1/2oz Monin Pear Syrup
- 1/2oz fresh lemon juice

Instructions:
1. Fill a martini shaker with ice.
2. Add the vodka, fig puree, syrup and lemon juice.
3. Shake until the ingredients are well blended and chilled, about 30 seconds.
4. Strain into a chilled martini glass.

Nutrition Information: (per serving)
- Calories: 149
- Protein: 0 g
- Fat: 0 g
- Sodium: 0.8 mg
- Total Carbohydrates: 14 g
- Sugars: 11.4 g

34. Honey Martini

An exquisite sweet and tart honey martini that will take your taste buds on a delightful journey.
Serving: Serve in a martini glass
Preparation time: 5 minutes
Ready time: 5 minutes

Ingredients:
- 2 ounces vodka
- 2 teaspoons honey
- 1/2 ounces lime juice
- 1/4 ounces triple sec

Instructions:
1. Fill a cocktail shaker with iced cubes.
2. Pour in vodka, honey, lime juice and triple sec.
3. Shake the mixture very well.
4. Strain into a martini glass.

Nutrition Information:
Serving Size: 1 martini | Calories: 148 kcal | Carbohydrates: 8.5 g | Protein: 0.1 g | Fat: 0.0 g | Saturated Fat: 0.0 g | Sodium: 0.1 mg | Potassium: 5.3 mg | Fiber: 0.1 g | Sugar: 8.4 g | Vitamin C: 0.6 mg | Calcium: 2.2 mg | Iron: 0.1 mg

35. Pomegranate Martini

This Pomegranate Martini is a delicious and unique drink that combines sweet, tart pomegranate juice with vodka and a splash of lime juice and simple syrup. It's fruity, refreshing, and surprisingly easy to make!
Serving: 1
Preparation Time: 5 minutes
Ready Time: 5 minutes

Ingredients:
- 2 ounces vodka
- 2 ounces pomegranate juice
- 1 ounce lime juice
- 1/2 ounce simple syrup
- Ice cubes
- Pomegranate arils (for garnish, optional)

Instructions:
1. Fill a cocktail shaker with ice.
2. Pour in vodka, pomegranate juice, lime juice, and simple syrup.
3. Shake vigorously for 15-20 seconds.
4. Strain into a chilled martini glass.
5. Garnish with pomegranate arils (optional).

Nutrition Information: (per serving)

Calories: 234 kcal; Carbohydrates: 12.4 g; Protein: 0.1 g; Fat: 0.1 g; Sodium: 1 mg; Sugar: 7 g.

36. Plum Martini

Plum Martini: This summertime drink is a fruity twist on the classic martini. It features juicy plums blended with vodka, Triple Sec and a splash of lemon juice for a tart but sweet sip.
Serving: 1
Preparation Time: 5 minutes
Ready Time: 5 minutes

Ingredients:
1 oz vodka
1 oz Triple Sec
1/4 cup plums, pureed
1/2 lemon, juiced
1/4 oz simple syrup

Instructions:
1. In a mixing tin, combine vodka, Triple Sec, plums, lemon juice, and simple syrup.
2. Fill with ice and shake vigorously until it's cold.
3. Strain into a chilled martini glass.
4. Garnish with a fresh plum, and serve.

Nutrition Information (per serving): 155 calories, 2.2 g fat, 0.3 g saturated fat, 0 g trans fat, 0 mg cholesterol, 1 mg sodium, 15 g carbohydrates, 0.7 g fiber, 11 g sugar, 0.5 g protein.

37. Rhubarb Martini

A classic Rhubarb Martini is a simple yet sophisticated option that will elevate any gathering. The combination of vodka, rhubarb juice, and elderflower liqueur create a delightful taste experience.
Serving: 1 Martini
Preparation Time: 5 minutes

Ready Time: 5 minutes

Ingredients:
- 2 ounces vodka
- 1 ounce rhubarb juice
- 1/2 ounce elderflower liqueur
- Ice

Instructions:
1. Add ice to a shaker, followed by vodka, rhubarb juice, and elderflower liqueur.
2. Shake vigorously for 30 seconds.
3. Strain the martini into a chilled martini glass.
4. Garnish with a strawberry or rhubarb twist.

Nutrition Information:
Calories: 140, Fat: 0g, Sodium: 0mg, Carbs: 6g, Protein: 0g

38. Melon Martini

This classic and refreshing Melon Martini is perfect for cocktail hour! This impressive and fruity drink is made with melon liqueur, vodka, and fresh lime.
Serving: Makes 1 drink
Preparation Time: 2 minutes
Ready Time: 2 minutes

Ingredients:
- 2 tablespoons melon liqueur
- 2 tablespoons vodka
- 1 teaspoon fresh lime juice

Instructions:
1. Fill a martini shaker or a large glass with ice.
2. Add melon liqueur, vodka, and fresh lime juice to the shaker or glass.
3. Shake or stir until all Ingredients are well combined.
4. Strain Martini into a chilled martini glass.
5. Enjoy!

Nutrition Information:
Calories: 147, Total Fat: 0 g, Sodium: 2 mg, Total Carbohydrate: 4 g, Protein: 0 g

39. Kiwi Martini

Kiwi Martini is a sweet and tart twist on the classic martini! Serves 2 people and takes 10 minutes of preparation time with an additional 5 minutes for chill time.
Serving: 2
Preparation Time: 10 minutes
Ready Time: 5 minutes

Ingredients:
- 2 ounces vodka
- 1/2 ounces dry vermouth
- 2 ounces kiwi puree
- 1 tablespoon sugar
- 1 teaspoon freshly-squeezed lime juice
- Kiwifruit slices, for garnish

Instructions:
1. In a shaker filled with ice, combine the vodka, dry vermouth, kiwi puree, sugar and lime juice.
2. Shake vigorously to combine.
3. Strain into two chilled martini glasses and garnish with kiwifruit slices.

Nutrition Information (per serving):
- Calories: 216
- Fat: 0 g
- Carbohydrates: 16 g
- Sugar: 10 g
- Protein: 1 g

40. Lychee Martini

Lychee Martini – the perfect combination of sweet and sour, this tantalizing martini is sure to impress.
Serving: Makes 1 drink
Preparation Time: 5 minutes
Ready Time: 5 minutes

Ingredients:
- 3 oz vodka
- 2 oz lychee juice
- 2 oz lime juice
- 1 tablespoon lychee syrup
- Lime wedges, for garnish

Instructions:
1. Fill a martini shaker with ice.
2. Pour vodka, lychee juice, lime juice, and lychee syrup into the martini shaker.
3. Shake well for 8-10 seconds.
4. Strain into a martini glass.
5. Garnish glass with a lime wedge and serve.

Nutrition Information: Per Serving – Calories: 147, Carbohydrates: 13g, Protein: 0g, Fat: 0g, Saturated Fat: 0g, Sodium: 0mg, Potassium: 27mg, Fiber: 0g, Sugar: 9g, Vitamin C: 9.5%, Calcium: 0.1%, Iron: 0.3%

41. Coconut Martini

This Coconut Martini is a delightfully delicious cocktail with a tropical beach flavor. It's simple to prepare and a perfect way to end a meal or to relax and cozy up with a friend.
Serving: Makes 1 Cocktail
Preparation Time: 5 minutes
Ready Time: 5 minutes

Ingredients:
- 2 ounces vodka
- 1 ounce coconut liqueur

- 1 ounce coconut cream
- Garnish with shredded coconut

Instructions:
1. Fill a shaker with ice cubes.
2. Pour in the vodka, coconut liqueur, and coconut cream and shake well.
3. Strain into a chilled martini glass.
4. Garnish with shredded coconut.

Nutrition Information: (Per Serving)
- calories: 192
- carbohydrates: 5g
- protein: 0.1g
- fat: 0.2g
- sodium: 2mg

42. Hazelnut Martini

Hazelnut Martini is a decadent and creamy concoction of vodka, Frangelico, and Half and Half. With just a few Ingredients and mixed in a matter of minutes, this martini is sure to become a favorite.
Serving: 1
Preparation time: 5 minutes
Ready time: 5 minutes

Ingredients:
- 2 ounces vodka
- 1 ounce Frangelico liqueur
- 2 ounces Half and Half

Instructions:
1. Fill a mixing glass with ice.
2. Add the vodka and Frangelico.
3. Stir for about 20 seconds.
4. Add the Half and Half.
5. Strain the contents into a martini glass.
6. Garnish with a few hazelnuts, if desired.

Nutrition Information:
Calories: 188; Fat: 2.3g; Cholesterol: 5.3 mg; Sodium: 1.7 mg; Carbohydrates: 0.7 g; Protein: 0.2 g.

43. Almond Martini

Almond Martini
Serving: 1
Preparation Time: 5 minutes
Ready Time: 5 minutes

Ingredients:
- 2 oz of vodka
- 1 oz of amaretto
- 1/2 oz of simple syrup
- 2 drops of almond extract
- 1/2 oz of heavy cream
- About 2 cups of crushed ice

Instructions:
1. In a cocktail shaker, combine all Ingredients except for the heavy cream.
2. Shake until the Ingredients are heavily combined and the ice is crushed.
3. Using a strainer, pour the mixture into a martini glass.
4. Top the drink with heavy cream. You can also add some crushed almonds as a garnish.
5. Serve and enjoy!

Nutrition Information:
Calories: 224
Fat: 5 g
Saturated Fat: 3 g
Carbohydrates: 14 g
Protein: 2 g
Cholesterol: 24 mg
Sodium: 10 mg
Fiber: 2 g

44. Pistachio Martini

Try something new with this creamy and delicious pistachio martini. This unique twist on a classic combines vermouth and pistachio ice cream with the classic vodka martini recipe. For an added touch, top with lightly toasted pistachio for a tasty garnish.
Serving: 1
Preparation time: 5 minutes
Ready time: 10 minutes

Ingredients:
- 1 oz vodka
- 1 oz vermouth
- 2 tablespoons pistachio ice cream
- Pistachio, for topping

Instructions:
1. In a cocktail shaker filled with ice, mix together vodka, vermouth and pistachio ice cream until combined.
2. Strain the mixture into a martini glass.
3. Garnish with lightly toasted pistachios.

Nutrition Information (per serving): 170 calories, 2.3g fat, 9.5g carbohydrates, 1.2g protein.

45. Walnut Martini

This summery Walnut Martini is sweet, nutty, and bursting with fresh flavor. It combines vodka and Frangelico to create the perfect balance of boozy sweetness.
Servings: 1
Preparation Time: 5 minutes
Ready Time: 5 minutes

Ingredients:
- 1½ ounces vodka

- 1½ ounces Frangelico
- ¼ ounce fresh lemon juice
- ½ ounce simple syrup
- Walnut pieces, for garnish

Instructions:
1. In a shaker filled with ice, add the vodka, Frangelico, lemon juice, and simple syrup.
2. Shake vigorously for 30 seconds.
3. Strain the martini into a glass.
4. Garnish with walnuts.

Nutrition Information:
Calories: 313, Fat: 1g, Sodium: 1mg, Carbohydrates: 16g, Protein: 1g, Sugar: 14g.

46. Maple Martini

Maple Martini
This sweet and creamy Maple Martini is the perfect indulgence for those seeking an elegant maple-infused cocktail. Perfect for special occasions or a cozy night in, you'll surely be pleased with this mouthwatering cocktail.
Serving: 1
Preparation Time: 5 minutes
Ready Time: 5 minutes

Ingredients:
- 2 ounces vodka
- 2 tablespoons pure maple syrup
- 1 ounces Triple sec
- 1 ounce cream
- 1/2 teaspoon ground cinnamon
- Lemon twist, for garnish

Instructions:
1. In a shaker filled halfway with ice, add the vodka, maple syrup, triple sec, cream, and cinnamon.

2. Shake vigorously for about 30 seconds.
3. Strain the martini into a chilled martini glass.
4. Garnish with a lemon twist.

Nutrition Information:
Calories: 143; Total Fat: 0.6g; Cholesterol: 2.6mg; Sodium: 1mg; Total Carbohydrates: 10.7g; Sugars: 6.1g; Protein: 0.5g

47. Bacon Martini

Bacon Martini: This sweet and savory delicious martini is made with bacon, vanilla vodka, maple whiskey, and ginger beer.
Serving: 2
Preparation Time: 10 minutes
Ready Time: 10 minutes

Ingredients:
- 2 strips of cooked bacon
- 2 ounces vanilla vodka
- 2 ounces maple whiskey
- 2 ounces ginger beer

Instructions:
- Cook the bacon strips until crisp. Set aside.
- Fill a shaker with ice.
- Pour in 2 ounces of vanilla vodka, 2 ounces of maple whiskey, and 2 ounces of ginger beer.
- Shake the Ingredients together until well blended.
- Strain the martini into 2 glasses.
- Garnish each glass with a bacon strip.

Nutrition Information:
- Calories: 258
- Fat: 13.8g
- Cholesterol: 25mg
- Sodium: 406mg
- Carbohydrates: 4.2g
- Protein: 7.6g

48. Mediterranean Martini

Mediterranean Martini: This zesty combination of vodka, dry vermouth, cucumber and olives is perfect for a warm summer evening.
Serving: 1
Preparation Time: 5 minutes
Ready Time: 5 minutes

Ingredients:
- 2 ounces vodka
- 1/2 ounce dry vermouth
- 1/2 small cucumber, cut into thin slices
- 3 pitted olives

Instructions:
1. Fill a shaker or large glass with ice cubes.
2. Pour in the vodka, dry vermouth, cucumber slices and olives.
3. Shake or stir for 30-45 seconds to mix and chill Ingredients.
4. Strain into a chilled martini glass or coupe glass.

Nutrition Information (per serving):
Calories: 116kcal, Carbohydrates: 2.7g, Protein: 0.6g, Fat: 0.2g, Sodium: 64mg, Sugar: 0.1g, Fiber: 0.5g

49. Mexican Martini

Mexican Martini
Serving: 1
Preparation Time: 5 minutes
Ready Time: 5 minutes

Ingredients:
- 2 fluid ounces silver tequila
- 2 fluid ounces orange liqueur
- 4 fluid ounces fresh lime juice
- 2 dashes orange bitters

- 2 teaspoons superfine sugar
- 2 cups ice cubes
- 1 lime wedge for garnish

Instructions:
Fill a cocktail shaker with the ice cubes. Add the tequila, orange liqueur, lime juice, orange bitters, and superfine sugar. Shake for 30 seconds or until the outside of the shaker gets cold. Strain the mixture into a martini glass and garnish with a lime wedge.

Nutrition Information:
Calories: 311, Fat: 0 g, Cholesterol: 0 mg, Sodium: 2 mg, Carbohydrates: 15 g, Protein: 0 g

50. Italian Martini

Italian Martini is a crisp and sophisticated spin on the classic martini. This easy drink is made with lightly sweetened limoncello, gin and dry vermouth and is certain to add an element of class to your next happy hour.
Serving: Makes 1
Preparation Time: 5 minutes
Ready Time: 5 minutes

Ingredients:
- 2 ounces gin
- 1 ounce Limoncello
- 1 ounce dry vermouth

Instructions:
1. Fill a cocktail shaker with ice.
2. Add gin, limoncello, and vermouth in the shaker.
3. Shake the Ingredients until chilled.
4. Strain the martini into a large martini glass.
5. Garnish with a lemon twist and serve.

Nutrition Information: (Per Serving) Calories: 198, Protein: 0 g, Carbohydrates: 4 g, Sodium: 0 mg, Fat: 0 g, Cholesterol: 0 mg, Sugar: 4 g

51. German Martini

The German Martini is a delicious and refreshing drink that is comprised of both gin and dry vermouth. This cocktail is easy to make and great for large gatherings.
Serving: 1
Preparation Time: 5 minutes
Ready Time: 5 minutes

Ingredients:
- 2 oz. gin
- 2 oz. dry vermouth
- 1-2 dashes orange bitters

Instructions:
1. Fill a shaker halfway with ice cubes.
2. Pour in the gin, dry vermouth, and orange bitters.
3. Shake the Ingredients until well-combined.
4. Strain the drink into a martini glass.
5. Garnish with an orange twist.

Nutrition Information: Per serving size of 1 martini there are approximately 170 calories with 0g of fat, 1g of protein, and 13g of carbohydrates.

52. Dutch Martini

Dutch Martini
Serving: 1
Preparation time: 5 minutes
Ready time: 5 minutes

Ingredients:

- 2/3 of Martini Bianco
- 2/3 of dry gin
- 1/3 of lemon juice
- 1/3 of orange juice

Instructions:
1. Fill a shaker or a tall glass with ice cubes.
2. Pour in 2/3 of Martini Bianco, 2/3 of dry gin, 1/3 of lemon juice, and 1/3 of orange juice in the glass or shaker.
3. Close the shaker (if any) and shake vigorously.
4. Strain the contents into a well-chilled coupe glass.
5. Serve and enjoy!

Nutrition Information:
Calories: 140 kcal, Sodium: 4mg, Total Fat: 0g, Total Carbohydrate: 3.7g, Protein: 0g

53. Japanese Martini

The Japanese Martini is an exotic twist on a classic martini drink that takes your taste buds on an adventure. This sweet and salty mix of cranberry juice and sake is a refreshing take on the classic is sure to tantalize the palate.
Serving: 1
Preparation Time: 5 minutes
Ready Time: 5 minutes

Ingredients:
2 ounces vodka
1 ounce sake
2 ounces cranberry juice
1/2 ounce lime juice

Instructions:
1. In a shaker filled with ice, combine vodka, sake, cranberry juice and lime juice.
2. Shake well and strain into a chilled martini glass.
3. Garnish with an orange twist.

Nutrition Information:
Calories – 175
Carbohydrates – 14 g
Fat – 0 g
Protein – 0 g
Sodium – 0 mg

54. Chinese Martini

Chinese Martini is an exotic martini that is inspired by the flavors of Chinese cuisine. It is a tempting balance of sweet and sour flavors that is sure to please any palate.

Serving: 1
Preparation Time: 5 minutes
Ready Time: 15 minutes

Ingredients:
-2 ounces vodka
-1/2 ounce Grand Marnier
-1/2 ounce orange juice
-1/4 ounce fresh lemon juice
-1 teaspoon honey

Instructions:
1. In a shaker filled with ice, combine vodka, Grand Marnier, orange juice, lemon juice and honey.
2. Shake well for 7-10 seconds.
3. Strain into a chilled cocktail glass.

Nutrition Information: (per serving)
Calories: 138 kcal, Carbohydrates: 11.7 g, Protein: 0 g, Fat: 0 g, Saturated Fat: 0 g, Polyunsaturated Fat: 0 g, Monounsaturated Fat: 0 g, Sodium: 0.6 mg, Potassium: 16 mg, Fiber: 0 g, Sugar: 9.1 g, Vitamin A: 0.3 %, Vitamin C: 8.2 %, Calcium: 1.2 %, Iron: 0.6 %

55. Indian Martini

Indian Martini is a classic martini recipe combined with the exotic flavors of India. It's sure to be a conversation starter at your next party!
Serving: 4
Preparation Time: 5 minutes
Ready Time: 5 minutes

Ingredients:
- 2 ounces vodka
- 1/2 ounce dry vermouth
- 2 to 3 cardamom seeds
- 1/4 teaspoon Indian bazaar spice blend

Instructions:
1. Combine the vodka, vermouth, and cardamom seeds in a shaker with ice.
2. Shake vigorously until well-chilled.
3. Strain into martini glasses and sprinkle a pinch of Indian bazaar spice blend over the top.

Nutrition Information:
Calories: 96, Fat: 0g, Saturated Fat: 0g, Carbs: 0g, Sugar: 0g, Protein: 0g

56. Thai Martini

Thai Martini is a distinct and delicious cocktail featuring a mix of fruity and herbal flavors. The traditional martini gets a bold twist with flavors of lemongrass, ginger, and Thai basil.
Serving: Makes one drink.
Preparation Time: 5 minutes
Ready Time: 5 minutes

Ingredients:
- 2 ounces vodka
- 0.5 ounces simple syrup
- 2 lemongrass stalks
- 2 slices of ginger

- 2 leaves of Thai basil (or Italian basil)
- Ice cubes

Instructions:
1. In a shaker, muddle together the lemongrass, ginger and basil.
2. Fill the shaker with ice and pour in the vodka and simple syrup.
3. Cover and shake vigorously for 10-15 seconds.
4. Strain into a martini glass and serve immediately.

Nutrition Information (per drink):
- 140 Calories
- 0 g Fat
- 0 g Cholesterol
- 0.2 g Sodium
- 12.7 g Carbohydrates
- 0.1 g Protein

57. Brazilian Martini

Brazilian Martini is an easy and delicious cocktail that combines lime juice, Cachaca or Crema de Tequila and sugar. It creates a drink that has a balance of sweet and tart with a hint of herbal
Serving: Makes 1
Preparation Time: 5 minutes
Ready Time: 5 minutes

Ingredients:
2 ounces Cachaca or Crema de Tequila
1 ounce lime juice
3/4 ounce simple syrup

Instructions:
1. Combine the Cachaca or Crema de Tequila, lime juice, and simple syrup in a shaker with ice.
2. Shake to combine and chill the drink.
3. Strain into a chilled glass.
4. Garnish with a wheel of lime, and serve.

Nutrition Information (per serving):
Calories: 250 kcal, Carbohydrates: 29 g, Fat: 0 g, Protein: 0 g, Sodium: 0.7 mg

58. Russian Martini

The Russian Martini is a simple twist on the classic Martini, made with vodka, vermouth and orange juice. It's a flavor packed drink sure to be a hit at any gathering.
Serving: 1
Preparation Time: 3 minutes
Ready Time: 3 minutes

Ingredients:
2 ounces vodka
1/2 ounce dry vermouth
1/2 ounce fresh orange juice

Instructions:
1. Fill a cocktail shaker with 3/4 cup ice.
2. Pour the vodka, vermouth and orange juice into the shaker and shake for 20-30 seconds.
3. Strain the mixture into a martini glass.
4. Garnish with an orange half wheel.

Nutrition Information: Calories: 188; Carbohydrates: 4 g; Protein: 0 g; Fat: 0 g; Sodium: 0 g; Sugar: 0 g.

59. Irish Martini

The Irish Martini is a creamy, smooth cocktail made with Irish whiskey, Irish cream, and half and half. This combination of Ingredients creates the perfect balance of flavors and makes for a delightful drink. It is often served as an after-dinner treat but is also great for sipping any time of day.
Serving: Makes 1 cocktail.
Preparation Time: 5 minutes

Ready Time: 5 minutes

Ingredients:
- 2 parts Irish whiskey
- 2 parts Irish cream
- 1 part half and half
- Ground coffee beans, for garnish

Instructions:
1. Fill a cocktail shaker halfway with ice cubes and add all the Ingredients.
2. Shake until everything is chilled and combined.
3. Strain the mixture into a martini glass and garnish with ground coffee beans.

Nutrition Information:
Calories: 188, Fat: 5.7 g, Sodium: 6.3 mg, Carbohydrates: 5.6 g, Protein: 0.2 g

60. Scottish Martini

The Scottish martini is a twist on the classic martini recipe that adds the smoky flavor of Scotch whisky for an extra kick. Enjoy this cocktail at events or as an after-dinner treat.
Serving: 1
Preparation Time: 5 minutes
Ready Time: 5 minutes

Ingredients:
-1½ teaspoons dry vermouth
-2½ ounces Scotch whisky, preferably a smoky single-malt variety
-2 dashes of orange bitters
-Ice
-Twist of orange peel, for garnish

Instructions:
1. Fill a cocktail shaker with ice and pour in the vermouth, whisky, and orange bitters.

2. Shake well, until it's chilled and all of the Ingredients are thoroughly mixed.
3. Strain the martini into a chilled cocktail glass.
4. Garnish with a twist of orange peel.

Nutrition Information: This recipe yields approximately 175 calories and has no fat or carbohydrates.

61. Caribbean Martini

This Caribbean Martini drink is the perfect blend of delicious tropical flavors! Smooth and creamy, this cocktail will transport you to an island oasis of fruity energy and excitement. It's the perfect way to relax and get away from it all.
Serving: 1
Preparation Time: 5 minutes
Ready Time: 5 minutes

Ingredients:
- 2 ounces golden rum
- 2 ounces cream of coconut
- 2 ounces pineapple juice
- 2 ounces orange juice
- 1 ounce grenadine syrup
- 1 lime, cut into wedges

Instructions:
1. In a shaker filled with ice, combine rum, cream of coconut, pineapple juice, orange juice and grenadine.
2. Shake the Ingredients vigorously until the shaker is thoroughly chilled.
3. Serve in a chilled martini glass and garnish with a wedge of lime.

Nutrition Information: Calories – 221, fat – 0, protein – 0, saturated fat – 0, carbs – 18 g, sugar – 16 g, sodium – 16 mg

62. African Martini

The African Martini is an exotic cocktail featuring earthy vodka, salty black olives, and sweet orange liqueur. This balanced libation is sure to tantalize the taste buds and make any drinker feel like they are in the heart of Africa.

Serving: 1 Drink
Preparation Time: 10 Minutes
Ready Time: 10 Minutes

Ingredients:
- 2 ounces Vodka
- ½ ounce CoIntreau or other orange liqueur
- 4 black olives

Instructions:
1. In a cocktail shaker filled with ice, combine the vodka and orange liqueur.
2. Shake to combine and very chill.
3. Strain the mixture into a chilled martini glass.
4. Garnish with four black olives.

63. American Martini

The American Martini is a cool and refreshing cocktail made with five simple Ingredients. It is a classic cocktail that is perfect for any occasion.

Serving: Makes 1 drink
Preparation Time: 5 minutes
Ready Time: 5 minutes

Ingredients:
- 2 ounces vodka
- 1 ounce dry vermouth
- 2 dashes of Angostura bitters
- Lemon twist, for garnish
- Maraschino cherry, for garnish

Instructions:
1. Fill a shaker with ice.

2. Pour the vodka, dry vermouth, and bitters into the shaker.
3. Shake the Ingredients until chilled.
4. Strain over an ice-filled rocks glass.
5. Garnish with a lemon twist and a maraschino cherry.

Nutrition Information:
Calories: 150
Total Fat: 0g
Saturated Fat: 0g
Cholesterol: 0mg
Sodium: 0mg
Total Carbohydrates: 0g
Dietary Fiber: 0g
Sugars: 0g
Protein: 0g

64. Asian Martini

Asian Martini
Serving: One
Preparation Time: 3 minutes
Ready Time: 3 minutes

Ingredients:
- 1 part vodka
- 2 parts lychee syrup
- 1 part lime juice
- Frozen lychee fruit, to garnish

Instructions:
1. Fill a shaker with ice.
2. Add the vodka, lychee syrup and lime juice into the shaker.
3. Shake the shaker vigorously for 15-30 seconds.
4. Strain the mixture into a chilled martini glass.
5. Garnish the drink with frozen lychee fruit.

Nutrition Information:
Calories: 122, Total Fat: 0g, Carbohydrates: 5g, Sugar: 4g, Protein: 0g

65. Oceanic Martini

Oceanic Martini is a sweet and salty cocktail that is perfect for any occasion. It combines the freshest flavor of the ocean with a combination of citrus and vodka. Serve this delicious and unique martini to your guests and they will sure to love it!
Serving: 2
Preparation Time: 5 minutes
Ready Time: 5 minutes

Ingredients:
- 4 oz Vodka
- 2 oz Blue Curaçao
- 1 Tbsp Capers
- 2 oz Lime Juice
- 2 oz Simple Syrup
- Splash of Soda Water

Instructions:
1. Fill a shaker with ice cubes.
2. Add vodka, Blue Curaçao, capers, lime juice, and simple syrup.
3. Shake vigorously for about 1 minute.
4. Strain into chilled glasses.
5. Top off with a splash of soda water and stir.

Nutrition Information:
Calorie: 181 kcal
Fat: 0g
Carbohydrate: 8.1g
Protein: 0g

66. Vegetarian Martini

This vegetarian martini is a light and refreshing way to finish any meal with a delicious twist. Its subtle flavors make it a great addition to any vegetarian cuisine.

Serving: Makes 1 serving.
Preparation Time: 5 minutes
Ready Time: 5 minutes

Ingredients:
- 2 ounces cucumber juice
- 1 teaspoon fresh lime juice
- 4 ounces vermouth
- 1 teaspoon of fresh chives
- 1 teaspoon celery salt

Instructions:
1. Blend cucumber juice, lime juice, and vermouth in a shaker.
2. Strain into a martini glass.
3. Garnish with fresh chives and celery salt.

Nutrition Information: Per serving: Calories: 172 Protein: 0g Fat: 0g Carbohydrates: 8g Sodium: 471g.

67. Vegan Martini

Delicious, refreshing and completely plant-based, the vegan martini is the perfect twist on the classic cocktail.
Serving: 1
Preparation Time: 5 Minutes
Ready Time: 5 Minutes

Ingredients:
- 1 ½ ounces vodka
- 1 ½ ounces vegan dry vermouth
- 2 teaspoon olive juice
- 1 olive (for garnish)

Instructions:
1. Begin by adding the vodka, vegan dry vermouth, and olive juice into a martini shaker.
2. Fill the shaker with ice and place the top on.
3. Shake the martini vigorously for 30 seconds.

4. After the martini is finished being shaken, strain it into a martini glass.
5. Garnish the vegan martini with an olive and serve.

Nutrition Information: Per martini: Calories 142, Total Fat 0g (Saturated 0g), Cholesterol 0mg, Sodium 6mg, Total Carbohydrate 1g (Dietary Fiber 0g), Protein 0g

68. Gluten-free Martini

This gluten-free martini is an easy and delicious cocktail that makes the perfect addition to any celebration. With only a few Ingredients and a minimal amount of preparation, you can whip this up in no time and enjoy a tasty and refreshing drink.
Serving: 1-2
Preparation Time: 5 minutes
Ready Time: 5 minutes

Ingredients:
2 parts vodka
1 part dry vermouth
Dash of olive juice
Ice

Instructions:
1. Fill a shaker with ice
2. Pour in vodka, dry vermouth, and olive juice
3. Shake for 20-30 seconds
4. Strain the martini into a coupe glass
5. Garnish with olives, if desired

Nutrition Information:
Calories: 127
Sodium: 2mg
Total Fat: 0g
Potassium: 0mg
Total Carbs: 0g
Protein: 0g

69. Low-carb Martini

Low-carb Martini: For those seeking a delicious low carb drink, this Martini is a great choice! Serve it with your favorite appetizers for a light and refreshing treat.
Serving: 1
Preparation Time: 5 minutes
Ready Time: 5 minutes

Ingredients:
- 2 ounces vodka
- 1 ounce chilled club soda
- 1 ounce sugar-free cranberry juice
- ½ ounce lime juice
- Optional garnish: Lime, Cranberries

Instructions:
1. Fill a shaker with ice.
2. Add vodka, club soda, cranberry juice, and lime juice.
3. Shake or stir vigorously.
4. Strain into a chilled martini glass.
5. Garnish with lime and cranberries (optional).

Nutrition Information (per serving):
Calories: 74 kcal, Carbohydrates: 2g, Protein: 0.03g, Fat: 0g, Saturated Fat: 0g, Sodium: 2.6mg, Potassium: 16.4mg, Sugar: 0g, Vitamin C: 1.3mg

70. Keto Martini

A Keto Martini is a low-carb take on the classic martini, perfect for those following a ketogenic diet.
Serving: 1 drink
Preparation Time: 10 minutes
Ready Time: 10 minutes

Ingredients:
- 2 ounces dry vermouth

- 2 ounces blanc vermouth
- 1/2 ounce juniper-flavored liquor (ie. dry gin)
- 2 tablespoons olive brine
- Celery stalks, for garnish

Instructions:
1. Combine the vermouths and juniper-flavored liquor in a shaker with 4-5 ice cubes.
2. Shake for 30 seconds until the Ingredients are well chilled.
3. Strain the mixture into a martini glass.
4. Top with the olive brine, and garnish with celery stalks.

Nutrition Information: Calories: 90, Fat: 0g, Protein: 0g, Carbohydrates: 0g, Sodium: 46mg.

71. Paleo Martini

Paleo Martini: This martini is made from vodka and flavored with fresh, tart cranberry juice. It is a delicious low-carb, gluten-free drink that everyone can enjoy.
Serving: 1
Preparation Time: 5 minutes
Ready Time: 5 minutes

Ingredients:
- 2 ounces vodka
- 2 ounces cranberry juice, fresh
- 2 dashes of orange bitters
- Ice cubes

Instructions:
1. Fill a cocktail shaker with ice cubes.
2. Pour in the vodka and cranberry juice.
3. Add the orange bitters.
4. Shake vigorously for about 30 seconds.
5. Strain into a martini glass.

Nutrition Information:

Calories: 125 kcal, Carbohydrates: 5 g, Protein: 0 g, Fat: 0 g, Saturated Fat: 0 g, Sodium: 9 mg, Sugar: 4 g

72. Dairy-free Martini

This dairy-free martini is a delicious and creamy solution for people who have a lactose-intolerance or avoid dairy products.
Serving: Serves 4
Preparation Time: 10 minutes
Ready Time: 10 minutes

Ingredients:
- 2 1/2 ounces of vodka
- 2 tablespoons of coconut milk
- 1/4 teaspoon of almond extract
- Ice

Instructions:
1. Fill a shaker with ice.
2. Pour in the vodka, coconut milk, and almond extract.
3. Shake until theMartini is nice and frothy.
4. Strain into Martini glasses.

Nutrition Information:
Calories: 95 Per Serving, Total Fat: 0g, Sodium: 3mg, Total Carbohydrates: 1g, Protein: 0g.

73. Nut-free Martini

Make a delicious and nut-free martini to indulge in a flavorful cocktail with a smooth finish.
Serving: 1
Preparation Time: 5 minutes
Ready Time: 5 minutes

Ingredients:
- 3 ounces vodka

- 1/2 teaspoon sugar-free simple syrup
- 3/4 ounce lemon juice
- Ice

Instructions:
1. In a cocktail shaker filled with ice, pour the vodka.
2. Add the sugar-free simple syrup and lemon juice.
3. Shake well for 30 seconds.
4. Pour the mixture into a chilled martini glass.

Nutrition Information:
Calories: 134; Fat: 0g; Cholesterol: 0mg; Sodium: 0mg; Carbohydrates: 1g; Sugar: 0g; Protein: 0g

74. Soy-free Martini

Soy-Free Martini: a delicious drink that combines vodka and sparkling cider for a unique and interesting flavor. Serves 1. Preparation time: 10 minutes. Ready in: 10 minutes.

Ingredients:
- 2 ounces vodka
- 2 ounces sparkling hard cider
- Ice

Instructions:
1. In a cocktail shaker filled with ice, combine the vodka and cider.
2. Shake and strain into a chilled martini glass.
3. Enjoy!

Nutrition Information:
- Calories: 143
- Carbohydrates: 8g
- Sodium: 6mg
- Protein: 0g
- Fat: 0g

75. Egg-free Martini

Enjoy a classic cocktail while skipping the egg white with this Egg-free Martini recipe!
Serving: Makes 1 drink
Preparation time: 5 minutes
Ready Time: 5 minutes

Ingredients:
- 2 parts dry gin
- 3/4 part dry vermouth
- 1/4 part orange liqueur
- 1/4 part fresh lemon juice
- Ice

Instructions:
1. Fill a martini shaker halfway with ice.
2. Pour the gin, dry vermouth, orange liqueur, and lemon juice over the ice.
3. Shake vigorously.
4. Strain the martini into a chilled martini glass.
5. Garnish with an orange peel if desired.

Nutrition Information: TBD

76. Grain-free Martini

Grain-free Martini is a delicious twist on the classic martini. It's the perfect drink for a special occasion or night out. This version uses a sugar-free, grain-free vodka to keep it light and guilt-free.
Serving: 1
Preparation time: 5 minutes
Ready time: 5 minutes

Ingredients:
- 2 oz grain-free vodka such as Primal Spirits
- 1 oz dry vermouth
- 2 olives (for garnish)

Instructions:
1. Fill a cocktail shaker with ice.
2. Pour in the grain-free vodka and dry vermouth.
3. Shake vigorously for 15 seconds and then strain into a martini glass.
4. Garnish with olives and serve immediately.

Nutrition Information: Per serving: 130 Calories, 0 g Total Fat, 0 g Cholesterol, 0 g Sodium, 0 g Total carbohydrates, 0 g Protein.

77. Sugar-free Martini

Sugar-free Martini
Serving: 1
Preparation time: 2 minutes
Ready time: 2 minutes

Ingredients:
- 2 ounces vodka
- 1 oz. dry vermouth
- 1 dash of lime juice
- Ice cubes

Instructions:
1. Add vodka, dry vermouth, and lime juice to a shaker filled with ice.
2. Shake the mixture vigorously until combined.
3. Strain martini into a chilled martini glass.
4. Garnish with a lemon twist if desired.

Nutrition Information: Serving size: 1; Calories: 162; Fat: 0g; Sodium: 0mg; Carbohydrates: 0g; Protein: 0g.

78. Non-alcoholic Martini

- Non-alcoholic Martini is a great way to enjoy a classic cocktail without the alcohol. This simple drink can be made with a range of ingredients such as lemonade, juice, and soda that will tantalize your taste buds.

Serving - 8
Preparation Time - 5 mins
Ready Time - 5 mins

Ingredients:
- 2 ounces of lemonade
- 2 ounces of cranberry juice
- 2 ounces of sprite or 7-Up
- Ice cubes
- Lemon wedges

Instructions:
1. Fill a shaker or a pint glass with ice.
2. Pour in the lemonade, cranberry juice and Sprite or 7-Up.
3. Cover the shaker or glass and shake vigorously for 15-20 seconds.
4. Strain the liquid into two martini glasses and garnish with lemon wedges.

Nutrition Information -
Calories - 146 kcal, Carbohydrates - 26 g, Protein - 0 g, Fat - 0 g, Sat Fat - 0 g, Cholesterol - 0 g, Sodium - 33 mg, Sugar - 26 g.

79. Mocktail Martini

Mocktail Martini: A non-alcoholic version of the classic martini, this refreshing and delicious drink is perfect for any occasion and sure to be a hit with both adults and children alike.
Serving: 2
Preparation Time: 5 minutes
Ready Time: 5 minutes

Ingredients:
- 1/3 cup of cranberry juice
- 1/3 cup of pomegranate juice
- 1/3 cup of orange juice
- 1/4 cup of pineapple juice
- 1/8 cup of lime juice
- Sugar or sweetener (optional)

Instructions:
1. In a mixing bowl, mix together the cranberry juice, pomegranate juice, orange juice, pineapple juice and lime juice until combined.
2. Pour the juice into two glasses. Add a pinch of sugar, or sweetener of choice, if desired.
3. Stir lightly, and serve.

Nutrition Information:
Calories: 148 calories; Carbohydrates: 36.9 g; Fat: 0 g; Protein: 1.3 g; Sodium: 15 mg.

80. Herbal Martini

Herbal Martini
Serving: 1
Preparation Time: 10 minutes
Ready Time: 10 minutes

Ingredients:
- 2 ounces vodka
- 1 teaspoon lemon verbena syrup
- 2 teaspoons elderberry liqueur
- 1 teaspoon fresh lemon juice
- Fresh lemon peel for garnish

Instructions:
1. In a shaker filled with ice, combine vodka, lemon verbena syrup, elderberry liqueur, and fresh lemon juice.
2. Shake vigorously until well combined and chilled.
3. Strain into a chilled martini glass.
4. Garnish with a fresh lemon peel.

Nutrition Information (Per Serving):
Calories: 115 kcal, Carbohydrates: 6 g, Protein: 0 g, Fat: 0 g, Sodium: 1 mg, Fiber: 0 g, Sugar: 5 g.

81. Floral Martini

Floral Martini: Enjoy the sweetness and fragrance of this aromatic floral-infused martini.
Serving: 2
Preparation Time: 5 minutes
Ready Time: 5 minutes

Ingredients:
- 2 shots of gin
- 1 ½ shots elderflower liqueur
- ½ shot of simple syrup
- 2 shots of fresh lime juice
- edible flowers (optional)
- Ice cubes

Instructions:
1. Fill a shaker with ice and add gin, elderflower liqueur, simple syrup and lime juice.
2. Place the lid on the shaker, shake vigorously for 10-15 seconds.
3. Strain the cocktail into two martini glasses.
4. Garnish each glass with edible flowers, if desired.

Nutrition Information: Not applicable.

82. Fruity Martini

Fruity Martini
Serving: 1
Preparation Time: 5 minutes
Ready Time: 5 minutes

Ingredients:
- 2 ounces vodka
- 1 ounce peach liqueur
- 1 ounce fresh orange juice
- 2 ounces pineapple juice
- ½ ounce simple syrup

- Orange wedge, for garnish

Instructions:
1. In a cocktail shaker, combine the vodka, peach liqueur, orange juice, pineapple juice, and simple syrup.
2. Fill the shaker with ice and shake vigorously until well blended.
3. Strain the drink into a martini glass.
4. Garnish with an orange wedge and serve.

Nutrition Information (per serving):
Calories: 261, Fat: 0g, Carbohydrates: 22g, Protein: 0g, Sodium: 5mg.

83. Nutty Martini

Nutty Martini:
Serving: 1
Preparation Time: 5 minutes
Ready Time: 5 minutes

Ingredients:
- 2 ounces of vodka
- 2 ounces of vanilla liqueur
- 1 ounce of hazelnut liqueur
- Chocolate shavings

Instructions:
1. Combine vodka, vanilla liqueur and hazelnut liqueur in a shaker filled with ice.
2. Shake Ingredients together vigorously and strain into a chilled martini glass.
3. Garnish with the chocolate shavings.

Nutrition Information:
Calories: 233; Total Fat: 0g; Sodium: 0mg; Total Carbohydrate: 5.2g; Sugars: 0.2g; Protein: 0g

84. Sweet Martini

This exotic and sweet martini will be sure to tantalize your taste buds! With its unique blend of flavors and colors, you'll be in for a treat!
Serving: 1 cocktail
Preparation Time: 5 minutes
Ready Time: 5 minutes

Ingredients:
- 1 ounce of orange liqueur
- 1 ounce of lime juice
- 2 ounces of vodka
- Crushed ice
- A long orange peel, for garnish

Instructions:
1. Fill a cocktail shaker with crushed ice.
2. Pour in the orange liqueur, lime juice, and vodka.
3. Shake vigorously for 15-20 seconds.
4. Strain the mix into a martini glass.
5. Garnish with a long orange peel.

Nutrition Information: 143 calories, 0 g fat, 0 g saturated fat, 0g carbohydrate, 0g protein, 0 g fiber

85. Sour Martini

Sour martini is a delicious classic martini recipe for a tasty cocktail.
Serving: Makes 1 Martini
Preparation Time: 5 Minutes
Ready Time: 5 Minutes

Ingredients:
2 ounces gin
¾ ounce lime juice
¾ ounce simple syrup

Instructions:

Fill a shaker with ice and add the gin, lime juice and simple syrup.
Shake vigorously for 30 seconds until well-chilled.
Fill a martini glass with fresh ice to chill.
Strain the mixture from the shaker into the chill martini glass.
Garnish with a lime wedge, if desired.

Nutrition Information:
Calories: 176, Fat: 0g, Saturated Fat: 0g, Cholesterol: 0mg, Sodium: 1mg, Carbohydrates: 7g, Fiber: 0g, Sugar: 6g, Protein: 0g

86. Salty Martini

Salty Martini
This tart and salty drink is perfect for a night of indulgence. With dry vodka shaken with saline solution, lemon juice, and olives for garnishing, this martini will have you wanting more.
Serving: 1
Preparation Time: 5 mins
Ready Time: 5 mins

Ingredients:
2 oz vodka
1/4 tsp salted solution
2 oz lemon juice
Olives, for garnish

Instructions:
1. Fill a shaker with ice and add vodka, salted solution, and lemon juice.
2. Shake and strain into a martini glass.
3. Garnish with olives and serve immediately.

Nutrition Information (per serving):
Calories: 166 kcal
Carbohydrates: 6.3g
Protein: 0.6g
Fat: 0g

87. Spicy Martini

Spice up your martini with this delicious spicy martini recipe! The sweetness of the cherry liqueur and orange liqueur pair perfectly with the kick of the Sriracha, making this martini perfect for any occasion.
Serving: 1
Preparation Time: 5 minutes
Ready Time: 5 minutes

Ingredients:
- 2 parts vodka
- 1 ½ parts cherry liqueur
- 1 ½ parts orange liqueur
- ½ part simple syrup
- 2 drops of sriracha
- Optional: Lime wedge for garnish

Instructions:
1) Combine the vodka, cherry liqueur, orange liqueur, and simple syrup in a shaker filled with ice.
2) Shake vigorously for 5-7 seconds.
3) Dip the rim of the martini glass in a small bowl of sriracha and lemon juice. To do this, simply turn the glass upside down and hold it over the bowl.
4) Strain the contents of the shaker into the prepared martini glass.
5) Add 2 drops of sriracha to the martini.
6) Garnish with a lime wedge, if desired.

Nutrition Information: Calories: 168; Fat: 0g; Carbohydrates: 6g; Protein: 0g.

88. Bitter Martini

Bitter Martini
Serving: 1
Preparation time: 5 minutes
Ready time: 5 minutes

Ingredients:
- 2 ounces chilled gin
- 1 ounce sweet vermouth
- ¾ ounce orange or grapefruit-flavored Italian bitter liqueur
- 1 orange twist, for garnish

Instructions:
1. Combine the gin, sweet vermouth, and Italian bitter liqueur in a martini shaker with plenty of ice.
2. Shake vigorously for 15-20 seconds, until chilled.
3. Strain the mixture into a chilled martini glass.
4. Garnish with a twist of orange or grapefruit.

Nutrition Information:
Calories: 121, Total Fat: 0g, Carbs: 2.1g, Protein: 0g

89. Umami Martini

Chase away the blues with this fruity and flavorful libation – the Umami Martini. Made with vodka, Aperol, orange juice, and a few dashes of MSG, this drink combines unique flavors that will leave you wanting more.

Serving: 1
Preparation Time: 5 mins
Ready Time: 5 mins

Ingredients:
- 2 oz. vodka
- 1 oz. Aperol
- 0.75 oz. orange juice
- 2 dashes of MSG

Instructions:
1. Combine vodka, Aperol, and orange juice into a shaker filled with ice.
2. Shake until all Ingredients are well combined.
3. Strain into a chilled martini glass and top with 2 dashes of MSG.
4. Garnish with a thin slice of orange.

Nutrition Information:
Calories: 122, Fat: 0g, Carbohydrates: 6.3g, Protein: 0g.

90. Dry Martini

The Dry Martini is a classic cocktail, easy to prepare and guaranteed to please.
Serving: 1
Preparation Time: 5 minutes
Ready Time: 5 minutes

Ingredients:
- 1 1/2 oz. gin
- 1/2 oz. dry vermouth
- Ice
- Lemon twist (for garnish)

Instructions:
1. Fill a cocktail shaker with ice.
2. Add gin and vermouth.
3. Shake for 30 seconds.
4. Strain into a chilled martini glass.
5. Garnish with lemon twist.

Nutrition Information: Not available as Nutrition Information will vary depending on the Ingredients used.

91. Extra Dry Martini

Extra Dry Martini is a classic, dry Martini made with gin and dry vermouth, and garnished with an olive or lemon twist. This easy cocktail is a classic after-dinner drink that can be served up or on the rocks.
Serving: 1
Preparation Time: 5 minutes
Ready Time: 5 minutes

Ingredients:
- 2 parts gin
- 1 part dry vermouth
- 1 olive or lemon twist for garnish

Instructions:
1. Fill a shaker halfway with ice.
2. Add 2 parts gin and 1 part dry vermouth to the shaker.
3. Stir the mixture well for about 10 seconds.
4. Strain the Martini into a chilled martini glass.
5. Garnish the glass with an olive or lemon twist.

Nutrition Information:
- Calories: 168
- Total Fat: 0 g
- Saturated Fat: 0 g
- Cholesterol: 0 mg
- Sodium: 2 mg
- Total Carbohydrates: 0 g
- Dietary Fiber: 0 g
- Sugars: 0 g
- Protein: 0.5 g

92. Very Dry Martini

Very Dry Martini
Serving: 1
Preparation Time: 5 minutes
Ready Time: 5 minutes

Ingredients:
- 3 ounces dry gin
- 1/2 ounce dry vermouth
- 1 lemon twist
- Ice cubes

Instructions:
1. Fill a martini shaker or large glass with ice.

2. Add the gin and vermouth.
3. Stir for about 30 seconds.
4. Strain into a martini glass.
5. Garnish with the lemon twist.

Nutrition Information:
Calories: 203 kcal, Protein: 0.3 g, Carbohydrates: 0.1 g, Fat: 0.2 g, Cholesterol: 0 mg, Sodium: 0 mg, Sugar: 0 g, Fiber: 0 g.

93. Bone Dry Martini

A Bone Dry Martini is a classic dry martini and is a great way to enjoy vodka or gin with a minimal amount of additional Ingredients.
Serving: Serves 1
Preparation Time: 5 minutes
Ready Time: 5 minutes

Ingredients:
- 2 oz vodka or gin
- 1 1/2 oz dry vermouth
- 2 ice cubes
- 2 olives

Instructions:
1. Fill a shaker halfway full of ice cubes.
2. Pour gin or vodka and vermouth in shaker.
3. Shake well.
4. Fill a martini glass with two olives.
5. Strain the contents of shaker into the glass.
6. Enjoy!

Nutrition Information: Not applicable

CONCLUSION

After going through this extensive cookbook, it is clear to see why the martini has stood the test of time as a staple in cocktail culture. The variety of recipes and ingredients showcased in this cookbook is impressive, ranging from classic, traditional martinis to bold and modern twists.

One of the most noteworthy aspects of this cookbook is how it manages to both honor and expand upon the martini. Each recipe highlights the unique characteristics of the drink, while also incorporating new flavors and techniques that bring it to new heights. From a classic gin martini to a chocolate espresso martini, there is truly something for everyone in this compilation.

Overall, "Shaken, not Stirred: 93 Martini Cocktail Recipes" is a well-rounded and comprehensive cookbook that any enthusiast of the martini will surely appreciate. The step-by-step instructions and beautifully photographed cocktails make it easy for both novice and experienced bartenders to follow, while the variety of recipes ensures that there is always something new to try.

In addition to the cocktail recipes, this cookbook includes helpful tips and tricks for creating the perfect martini, from selecting the right spirits and mixers to choosing the perfect glassware. It is clear that the authors have put a lot of thought and care into crafting this cookbook, making it a valuable resource for anyone looking to take their martini game to the next level.

Ultimately, whether you are a martini aficionado or a newcomer to the world of cocktails, "Shaken, not Stirred: 93 Martini Cocktail Recipes" is a must-have addition to any bar or kitchen. With its wide range of recipes and expert advice, this cookbook is sure to impress and satisfy even the most discerning of martini drinkers. So why not shake things up and give some of these delicious recipes a try? It's time to get creative and see what new and exciting twists you can put on this timeless classic. Cheers!

Made in United States
North Haven, CT
22 December 2024